Analysis of suitable generative algorithms for the
generation of safety-critical driving data in the field
of autonomous driving

Analysis of suitable generative algorithms for the generation of safety-critical driving data in the field of autonomous driving

Nico Schick

Bibliografische Information der Deutschen Nationalbibliothek

Die Deutsche Nationalbibliothek verzeichnet diese Publikation in der Deutschen Nationalbibliografie; detaillierte bibliographische Daten sind im Internet über http://dnb.d-nb.de abrufbar.

1. Aufl. - Göttingen: Cuvillier, 2021

© CUVILLIER VERLAG, Göttingen 2021
  Nonnenstieg 8, 37075 Göttingen
  Telefon: 0551-54724-0
  Telefax: 0551-54724-21
  www.cuvillier.de

  ISBN 978-3-7369-7453-1
  eISBN 978-3-7369-6453-2

Analysis of suitable generative algorithms for the generation of safety-critical driving data in the field of autonomous driving

Nico Schick*

Machine learning algorithms are being increasingly used in the field of autonomous driving. For example, generative algorithms can be used to generate time series corresponding to safety-critical driving scenarios. This paper answers the following scientific question:

Which generative algorithms are particularly suitable for generating time series appropriate for the study of autonomous driving?

Keywords: Autonomous driving, safety-critical driving scenarios, time series, generative algorithms, Generative Adversarial Network (GAN), Restricted Boltzmann Machine (RBM), Recurrent Neural Network (RNN), Conditional Restricted Boltzmann Machine (CRBM), Factored Conditional Restricted Boltzmann Machine (FCRBM), Recurrent Temporal Restricted Boltzmann Machine (RTRBM), Variational-Autoencoder Generative Adversarial Network (VAE-GAN), Recurrent-Conditional Generative Adversarial Network (RCGAN), Time-Series Generative Adversarial Network (TimeGAN)

I. Motivation

Approximately 3700 people die in traffic accidents each day [1] [2] [3] [4] [5]. The most frequent cause of accidents is human error [6]. Autonomous driving can significantly reduce the number of traffic accidents. To prepare autonomous vehicles for road traffic, the software and system components must be thoroughly validated and tested. However, due to their criticality, there is only a limited amount of data for safety-critical driving scenarios. Such driving scenarios can be represented in the form of time series. These represent the corresponding kinematic vehicle movements by including vectors of time, position coordinates, velocities, and accelerations. There are several ways to provide such data. For example, this can be done in the form of a kinematic model. Alternatively, methods of artificial intelligence or machine learning can be used. These are already being widely used in the development of autonomous vehicles. For example, generative algorithms can be used to generate safety-critical driving data. A novel taxonomy for the generation of time series and suitable generative algorithms will be described in this paper. In addition, a generative algorithm will be recommended and used to demonstrate the generation of time series associated with a typical example of a driving-critical scenario.

---

*N. Schick, M. Sc. studied Applied Computer Sciences (M. Sc.) and Computer Engineering (B. Eng.) at the Esslingen University of Applied Sciences. e-mail: Nico.Schick@hs-esslingen.de

II. Time Series

Sequential data represents an ordered list of events. This type of data can be found in various use cases, such as in biology (e.g. DNA or protein sequences) or symbolic sequences (e.g. logical sequences of a customer purchase). Another important type of sequential data are time series. These contain numerical data, typically with a fixed and discrete time interval. Time series are found in a wide variety of applications. These occur in nature, in the form of temperature or climate, and in economics, in the form of stock prices. Sensor data of vehicles are also time series. With the help of time series analysis, the structure of time series can be understood. [6] [7]

III. Generative Algorithms

Generative algorithms belong to the field of machine learning and have gained significant attention in recent years. This type of algorithm can be understood as the counterpart to discriminative algorithms. They can, based on a probability distribution, generate new data. For this, information about the characteristics of the features are needed. In this regard, the characteristics of the different observations from the original data set, respectively, training data set, are transformed into a probability model. In the course of a stochastic process, the generative algorithm approximates a probability distribution of the training data set. The training phase of the probability model can be considered complete as soon as the generated data hardly differ from the original data set. Classical generative algorithms do not require labeled data sets (unsupervised learning). However, there are also mixed forms, which also depend on labels (unsupervised and supervised learning). [8] [9] A closer look at the literature reveals a higher-level taxonomy of generative algorithms in general. [8]

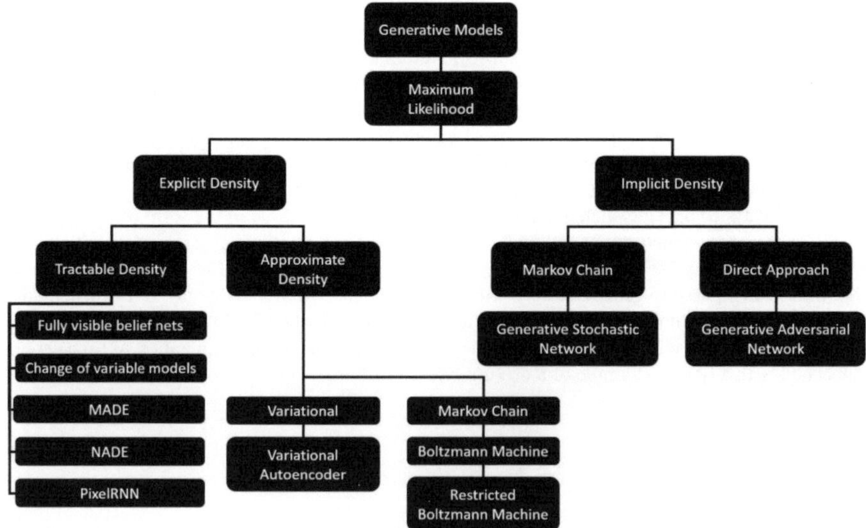

Fig. 1   Taxonomy of generative models

As seen in Figure 1, all generative algorithms are derived from the maximum likelihood method. A basic classification into explicit and implicit densities is made. Here, density refers to the probability density function (PDF) of the data set. The term 'explicit density' refers to an explicit or a closed expression of such a PDF. The implicit density method, on the other hand, estimates the PDF during the training phase. The explicit approach distinguishes between tractable densities and approximate densities. Generative algorithms, which belong to the group of tractable density, can be executed in polynomial time. These include algorithms such as Fully visible belief nets, Neural Autoregressive Distribution Estimation (NADE), Masked Autoencoder for Distribution Estimation (MADE), Pixel Recurrent Neural Networks (PixelRNN) or change of variable models. With generative algorithms, which instead belong to the group of approximate densities, a known PDF is approximated during the training phase. In particular, the Variational Autoencoder (VAE) as well as the Restricted Boltzmann Machine (RBM) are to be mentioned in this regard. VAEs were one of the first known generative neural networks of their kind. They are used in the field of image processing and feature reduction. RBMs are an extension of the Boltzmann Machines. They are used, for example, in the generation of human motion sequences. With the implicit approach, a subdivision between Generative Stochastic Networks (GSN) and Generative Adversarial Networks (GAN) takes place. GSNs are Markov chains and mimic the Gipps sampler of a Depp Boltzmann Machine. They can handle sequential data, but are not suitable for time series. [8] [9]

A. Generative Adversarial Networks

Generative Adversarial Networks (GAN) have gained great popularity in recent years. Moreover, they have been able to achieve continual improvement in their quality. The range of applications for GANs is diverse. GANs are used in different domains, such as image, video, audio, text, speech processing as well as time series. Goodfellow et al. developed the first concept of GAN in 2014. According to Figure 1, GANs determine a PDF in an implicit-direct manner. In more detail, a stochastic procedure is defined that is capable of generating synthetic data directly. The generation of new synthetic data is based on existing data sets. The basic structure of a GAN model consists of two artificial neural networks (ANNs), the so-called generator (G) and the discriminator (D), which perform a zero-sum game. [8] [9] The structure of the model is illustrated in Figure 2.

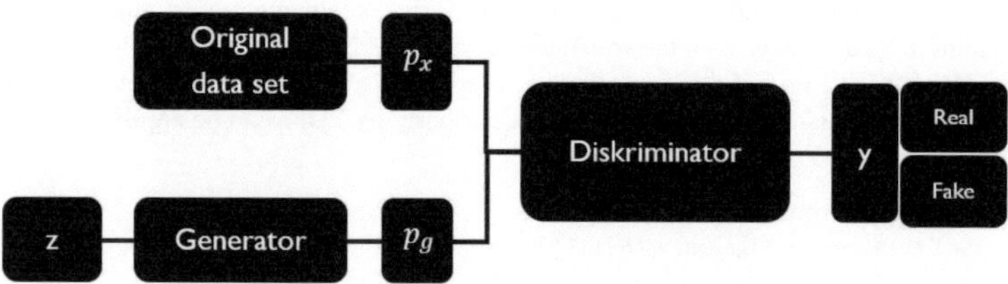

Fig. 2   Structure of a GAN model [8]

The task of the generator is to generate new synthetic data, whereas these data are evaluated or criticized by the discriminator. At the beginning, a probability distribution p_x is generated from an original data set, respectively, a training data set. It is used for representing the features of the original data set x in a latent space (sub-space). At first, the generator is initialized with a latent random vector z. The goal of the generator is to learn to generate synthetic data, according to an approximate distribution (p_g). The discriminator, on the other hand, tries to distinguish between the generated data and the original data. Here, y indicates whether x comes from p_x (with $y = 1$) or from p_g (with $y = 0$). GANs include white noise at the beginning of the training exclusively. Both networks interact with each other until the generator generates synthetic data that cannot be distinguished by the discriminator from the original data. This process is also known as a minimax game (also a zero-sum game), where the loss function of the discriminator is maximized and that of the generator is minimized. The total loss function $V(G, D)$ is defined as follows: [8] [9]

$$\min_{G} \max_{D} V(G, D) = \mathbb{E}_{x \sim p_{data}(x)} \left[\log D(x) \right] + \mathbb{E}_{z \sim p_z(z)} \left[\log(1 - D(G(z))) \right] \tag{1}$$

During training, the GAN model is optimized alternately. This involves fixing the weights of one network while optimizing the weights of the other one, and vice versa. At the beginning of the training, the generator is fixed first, to adjust the weights of the discriminator. Then, the weights of the discriminator are fixed, to update those of the generator. This process is repeated at each training iteration until the distribution of the synthetic data set p_g resembles the original data set p_x. After several training steps, the generator and discriminator reach a state where neither can improve. In this way, the global optimum is reached as soon as p_g and p_x are identical. This means that the discriminator can no longer distinguish between those two distributions. This is achieved as soon as $D(x) = 0.5$. Afterwards, the training phase is terminated and the discriminator is discarded. The discriminator has fulfilled its task by helping the generator to reach its target distribution ($p_g = p_x$) in order to be able to generate new data based on the approximation p_g. GANs are characterized by the high quality of the generated data. The diversity of applications is to be emphasized also. Due to the explosive nature of GANs, it is expected that this type of algorithm will continue to improve. There are already many publications about GANs. The tendency is still increasing. The training phase of a GAN is considered as a major challenge. It is mathematically complex and can lead to consequent numerical instabilities. The reason for this is the already mentioned minimax problem of the loss function. The evaluation of the generated data of a GAN is difficult to implement. Currently, expert knowledge (qualitative consideration) is used in this regard, for example. Alternatively, similarity measures (quantitative consideration) of underlying PDFs can be applied also. [8] [9]

B. Restricted Boltzmann Machines

Restricted Boltzmann Machines (RBM) belong to the group of generative algorithms that represent an explicit probability model. An RBM is an ANN consisting of a visible layer and a hidden layer. They have the ability to learn a probability distribution of the original data set. RBMs were developed in 1985 by Hinton and Sejnowski. They can be used for dimensionality reduction, classification, regression, collaborative filtering, feature learning, topic modeling, as well as sequences. They are an extension of Boltzmann machines and are constrained with respect to the connections between the visible and hidden nodes. [8] The abstract structure of an RBM model is shown in Figure 3.

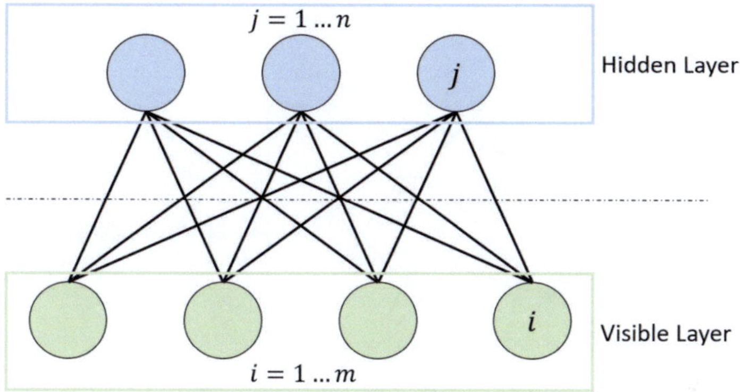

Fig. 3   Structure of an RBM model [8]

The graph illustrates a bipartite undirected graph. This consists of m visible units as well as n hidden units. Each node in the visible layer is connected to each node in the hidden layer. However, due to the constraint, nodes in the same layer are not connected to each other. This allows the use of efficient and numerically more stable training algorithms, such as the gradient-based Contrastive Divergence (CD) algorithm. RBMs approximate a distribution function stochastically. The joint probability distribution of the model is given by the Gibbs distribution [8]

$$p(v, h) = \frac{1}{Z} e^{-E(v,h)} \tag{2}$$

with the loss fuction [8]

$$E(v, h) = - \sum_{i=1}^{n} \sum_{j=1}^{m} w_{ij} h_i v_j - \sum_{j=1}^{m} b_j v_j - \sum_{i=1}^{n} c_i h_i \tag{3}$$

Here w_{ij} denotes the weight of the connection between units v_i and h_j. The visible units v_i represent observable data, whereas the hidden units capture the dependencies between the observed variables. There are two different bias units (hidden and visible biases). The hidden biases c_i are used in the forward pass and the visible biases b_j to reconstruct the input during the backward pass. The variable Z denotes the distribution function and is given by summing over all possible pairs of visible and hidden vectors: [8]

$$Z = \sum_{v,h} e^{-E(v,h)} \tag{4}$$

The forward pass respectively the training of the network is shown in Figure 4 with several inputs x.

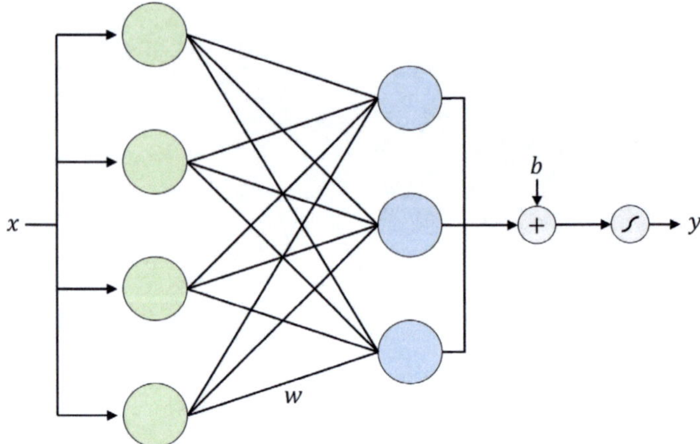

Fig. 4　Forward pass of an RBM model [8]

In the first step, the inputs x are multiplied by the weights w_i and then added with the bias b_j. The output is then passed through a sigmoid activation function. The output determines whether the hidden node is activated or not (binary activation). The weights represent a matrix, with the number of input nodes (number of rows), and the number of hidden nodes (number of columns). Before the bias value is added to the first hidden node, a vector multiplication of the inputs multiplied by the first weight column is applied. [8]

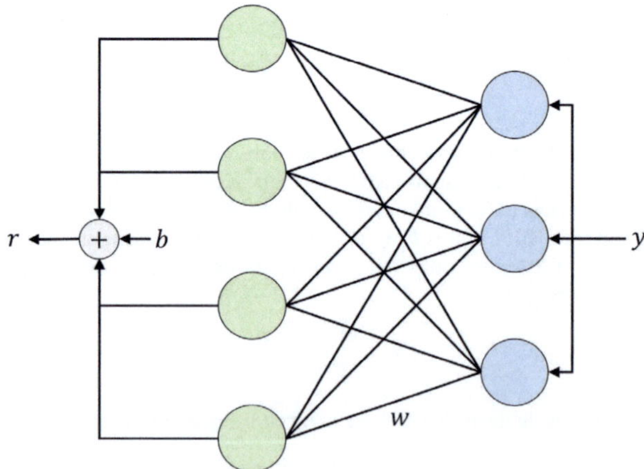

Fig. 5　Backward pass of an RBM model [8]

Once the training has been completed, the backward pass follows. Figure 5 shows its structure. While the RBM uses inputs to predict node activations during the forward pass, it tries to estimate the probability of inputs during the backward pass based on given activations. The difference between the reconstructions and the original input is due to the random initialization of the weights applied at the beginning. This is also referred to as reconstruction error, and is the difference between the reconstructed values r and the original input values x. In an iterative learning process, this error is used to optimize the weights of the network until a minimum error is reached. To measure the distance between two PDFs, RBMs use the Kullback–Leibler divergence. The CD is used to minimize the distance of both probability distributions accordingly. RBMs are more efficient and numerically stable compared to the unconstrained Boltzmann machine, due to their constraints as well as in conjunction with the CD algorithm applied. Those RBMs which contain recurrent nodes use LSTM cells mostly to build-up the recurrent behaviour accordingly. This promotes the information flow of the hidden units. [8]

IV. Recurrent Neural Networks

Recurrent Neural Networks (RNNs) are known in the modeling of sequence data due to their recurrent characteristics. By preserving past information over time, RNNs are able to learn the temporal properties of the original data set. RNNs have applications in language translation, speech generation, handwriting recognition, image-to-text translation, and machine translation. [8] [9] The general structures of a standard neural network and those of an RNN model are illustrated in the following.

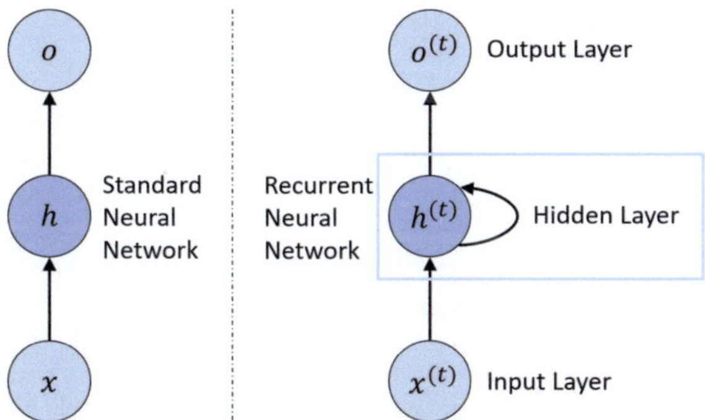

Fig. 6   General structures of standard neural network and of an RNN model [8]

In Figure 6 both networks have only one hidden layer. In this simplified representation, not all units of the input layer x, hidden layer h, and the output layer o are illustrated. In contrast to a standard feed forward neural network, in an RNN the hidden layer receives two inputs. These include the values from the current input layer as well as from the hidden layer (from the previous time step $t - 1$). Such an information flow is represented in the model as a loop, which is also referred to as a recurrent edge. [8] [9] For a closer look at the information flow, an unfolded representation of an RNN model is illustrated in Figure 7.

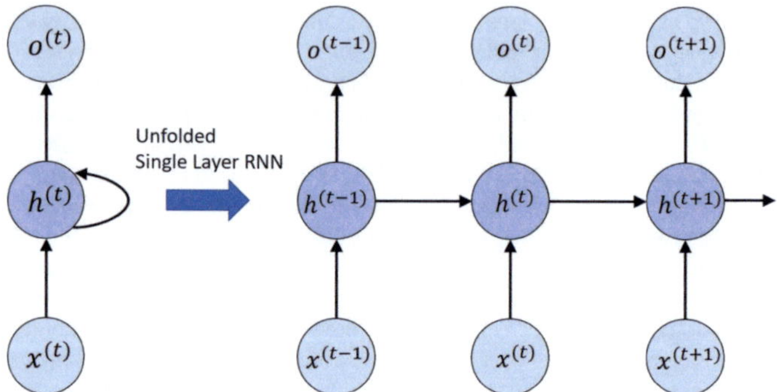

Fig. 7   Unfolded representation of an RNN [8]

At the beginning of the training, the hidden units are initialized with zeros or small random values. In Figure 8, different weight matrices of a standard RNN are shown.

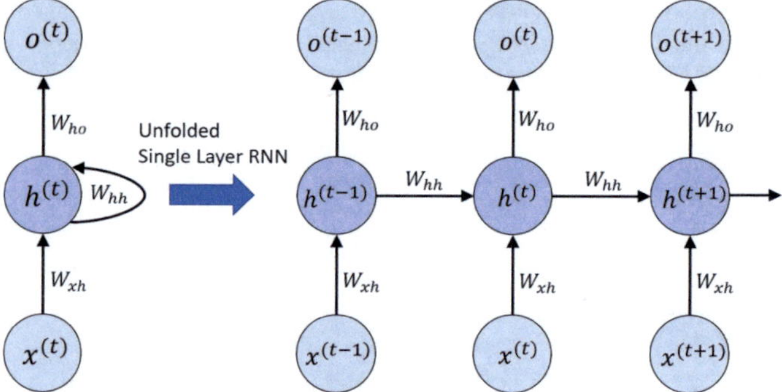

Fig. 8   Weight matrices of an RNN [8]

The directed edges between units are associated with weights, making up a weight matrix. These weights are independent of time. There are several different weight matrices in a single-layer RNN, as listed below: [8] [9]

- W_{xh}: The weight matrix between the input layer and the hidden layer.
- W_{hh}: The weight matrix associated with the recurrent edge.
- W_{ho}: The weight matrix between the hidden layer and the output layer.

The calculation of the activations of an RNN model is described in more detail below. For the hidden layer, the network input z_h (pre-activation) is calculated by a linear combination from adding the sum of the multiplications of the weight matrices with the corresponding vectors to the bias vector b_h: [8] [9]

$$z_h^{(t)} = W_{xh}x^{(t)} + W_{hh}h^{(t-1)} + b_h \tag{5}$$

The activations of the hidden units at time step t are calculated as follows: [8] [9]

$$h^{(t)} = \phi_h\left(z_h^{(t)}\right) = \phi_h\left(W_{xh}x^{(t)} + W_{hh}h^{(t-1)} + b_h\right) \tag{6}$$

The size b_h is the bias vector for the hidden units and ϕ_h is the activation function of the hidden layer. Once the activations of the hidden units at the current time step are calculated, the activations of the output units are determined as follows: [8] [9]

$$o^{(t)} = \phi_o\left(W_{ho}h^{(t)} + b_o\right) \tag{7}$$

The variable ϕ_o is the activation function and b_o is the bias vector of the output layer. The training phase of an RNN is a major challenge in general. This refers especially to the recurrent edges. During the computation of the gradients, the so-called vanishing gradient problem and exploding gradient occur. These are shown by the examples in Figure 9.

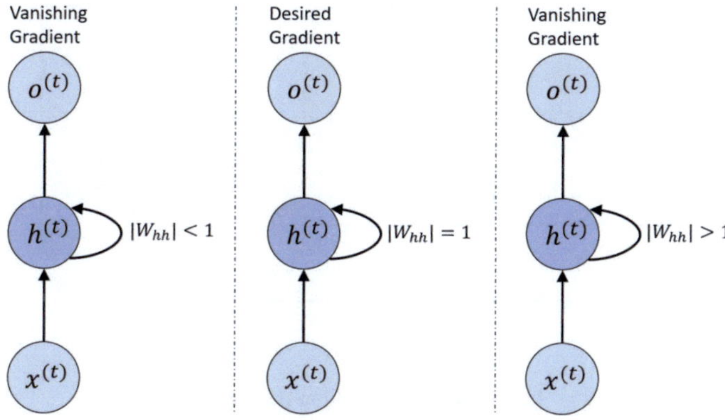

Fig. 9   Vanishing and Exploding problem [8]

Basically, the network has $t - k$ multiplications. Therefore, multiplying the weight w by itself, results in a factor w_{t-k} for $t - k$ times. When $|w| < 1$, this factor takes a very small value (vanishing) if $t - k$ is large. On the other hand, in case the weight of the recurrent edge is $|w| > 1$, then the factor w_{t-k} becomes very large (exploding) if $t - k$ is large also. Such a high value of $t - k$ is present in case the underlying data have larger lengths. A solution to avoid vanishing or exploding gradients can be achieved by ensuring $|w| = 1$. There are at least three different approaches, as listed below: [8] [9]
- Gradient Clipping (GC)
- Truncated Backpropagation over Time (TBPTT)
- Long Short Term Memory (LSTM)

GC is used to specify a threshold value for the gradients: gradients that exceed this value are rescaled to produce a more plausible behaviour of the gradient descent. In contrast, TBPTT limits the number of time steps that the signal can backpropagate after each forward pass. However, such a truncation approach limits the number of steps that the gradient can effectively flow back and update the weights properly. [8] [9]

LSTM cells, on the other hand, are able to successfully counteract such gradient problems efficiently, also when dealing with larger data sets. The building block of an LSTM include a memory cell that essentially replaces the hidden layer of a standard RNN. In each memory cell, there is a recurrent edge that has the desired weight $w = 1$. The values associated with this recurrent edge are collectively referred to as the cell state. [8] [9] The unfolded structure of a modern LSTM cell is shown in Figure 10.

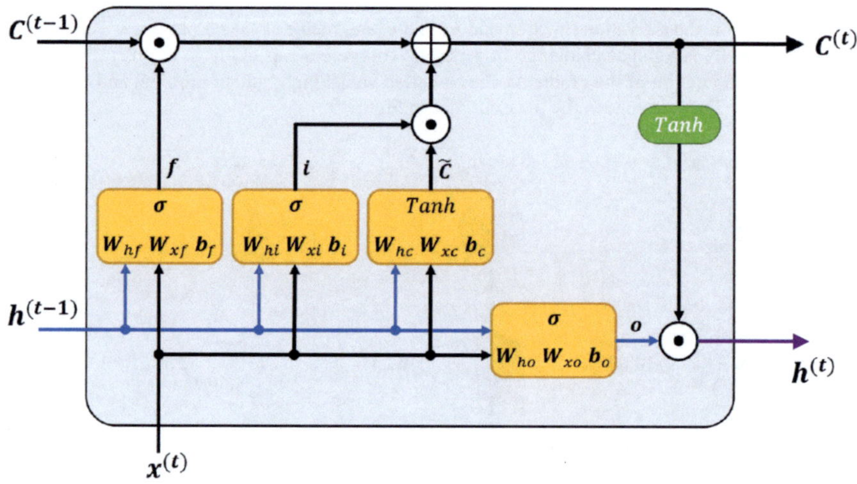

Fig. 10   LSTM cell of the hidden unit of an RNN [8]

To obtain the cell state at the time step $C^{(t)}$, the cell state from the previous time step $C^{(t-1)}$, without being directly multiplied by a weight factor, is updated. The information flow in this memory cell is affected by several computational units. In Figure 10, the sign $\odot$ refers to element-wise multiplication and $\oplus$ to element-wise addition. The size $x^{(t)}$ refers to the input data at time t and $h^{(t-1)}$ refers to the hidden units at time $t - 1$. The four yellow blocks are each characterized by either a sigmoid or tanh activation function, as well as a series of weights. These computational units carry out a linear combination by performing matrix–vector multiplications on their inputs $h^{(t-1)}$ and $x^{(t)}$. They are likewise referred to as gates. In an LSTM cell, there are three different types of gates: forget gate, input gate, and output gate. [8] [9]

A forget gate f_t allows the memory cell to reset the cell state without growing indefinitely. More specifically, a forget gate decides what kind of information to pass through and what kind of information to suppress. It is calculated as follows: [8] [9]

$$f_t = \sigma \left(W_{xf} x^{(t)} + W_{hf} h^{(t-1)} + b_f \right) \tag{8}$$

The input gate i_t and the candidate value $\tilde{C}_t$ are responsible for updating the cell state. They are determined as follows: [8] [9]

$$i_t = \sigma \left(W_{xi} x^{(t)} + W_{hi} h^{(t-1)} + b_i \right) \tag{9}$$

$$\tilde{C}_t = \tanh \left(W_{xc} x^{(t)} + W_{hc} h^{(t-1)} + b_c \right) \tag{10}$$

The cell state at time t is defined as follows: [8] [9]

$$C^{(t)} = \left(C^{(t-1)} \odot f_t \right) \oplus \left(i_t \odot \tilde{C}_t \right) \tag{11}$$

The output gate o_t decides how the values of the hidden units are updated: [8] [9]

$$o_t = \sigma \left(W_{xo} x^{(t)} + W_{ho} h^{(t-1)} + b_o \right) \tag{12}$$

Finally, the hidden units at the current time step are calculated as follows: [8] [9]

$$h^{(t)} = o_t \odot \tanh \left(C^{(t)} \right) \tag{13}$$

V. Taxonomy of generative algorithms for the generation of time series

Compared to Chapter III, there is a variety of different types of generative algorithms. Accordingly, there is also a large number of sub-variants. For example, there are over 500 different variants of GAN [10]. For the use case in the present context, focusing on the generation of time series, the generative algorithms of the types GAN and RBM are more relevant. Based on a detailed literature review, a novel taxonomy can be derived accordingly. This taxonomy contains six generative algorithms which are able to generate appropriate time series. For this reason, those generative algorithms are described in more detail below. [8]

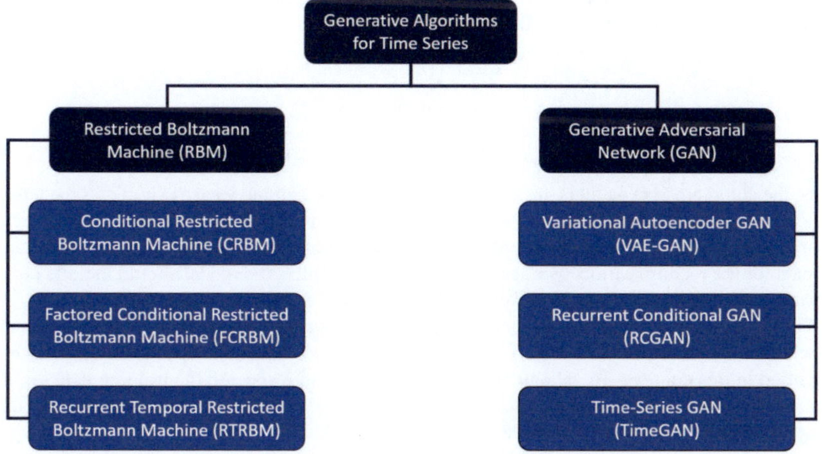

Fig. 11   Taxonomy of generative algorithms with respect to time series [8]

A. Conditional Restricted Boltzmann Machines

The Conditional Restricted Boltzmann Machine (CRBM) is a type of RBM that includes an additional conditional part. CRBMs are used, for example, for the generation of synthetic human motion sequences. By adding the conditional input, it is possible to model temporal dependencies. In more detail, the n past time units of the visible layer are fed to the hidden layer.

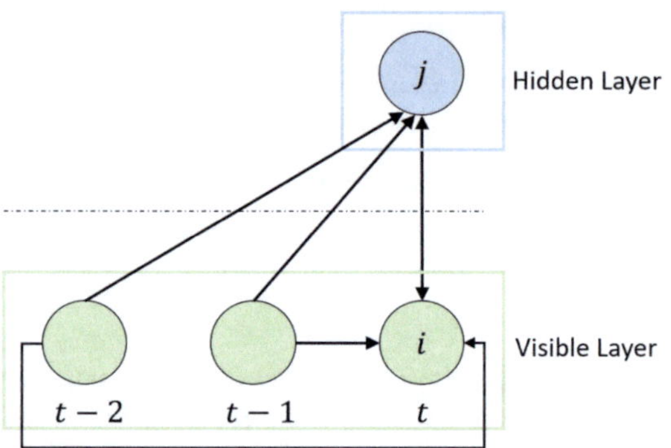

Fig. 12   Structure of a CRBM (simplified)

CRBMs contain n autoregressive directed graphs. Figure 12 shows an example of a CRBM for $n = 2$. There are connections from the past visible time steps to the current hidden layer. By adding the additional directed connection, a classical RBM is transformed to a CRBM. To train the model, the CD algorithm is used in a slightly modified version. Thus, the training algorithm also includes the dynamically changing biases of the hidden units (h):

$$\Delta d_{ij}^{(t-q)} \propto v_i^{t-q} \left(\langle h_j^t \rangle_{data} - \langle h_j^t \rangle_{recon} \right) \tag{14}$$

Similarly, the training algorithm for the visible units is (v):

$$\Delta a_{ki}^{(t-q)} \propto v_k^{t-q} \left(v_i^t - \langle v_i^t \rangle_{recon} \right) \tag{15}$$

Using the autoregressive weights, the temporal time units are well modeled. This allows the hidden units to abstract longer term structures at a higher level. The hidden units use stochastically selected binary values. Thus, the hidden activities do not use an unlimited amount of information from the data for the reconstruction. For accurate temporal inference, the model should include both a forward and a backward pass. However, it should be noted that an undefined backward pass can lead to training instabilities in undirected models. Through the autoregressive connections, the associated time units are overlaid with a continuous uniform distribution. Specifically, white noise is applied in this context. To validate the generated data with respect to the training data set, the nearest-neighbour interpolation algorithm can be used. CRBMs have several advantages. The data do not need to be heavily preprocessed. Accordingly, a reduction of the feature dimensions is not necessary. The inference of the generated data is of good quality. By observing the states of the visible entities, the hidden entities become conditionally independent. The model is also able to efficiently replace missing data in the training data set. [8] [11]

B. Factored Conditional Restricted Boltzmann Machines

The Factored Conditional Restricted Boltzmann Machine (FCRBM) is an RBM that includes a conditional part with factorized weights. Thus, FCRBMs can be considered as an extension of CRBMs. FCRBMs can also be used for the generation of synthetic human motion sequences.

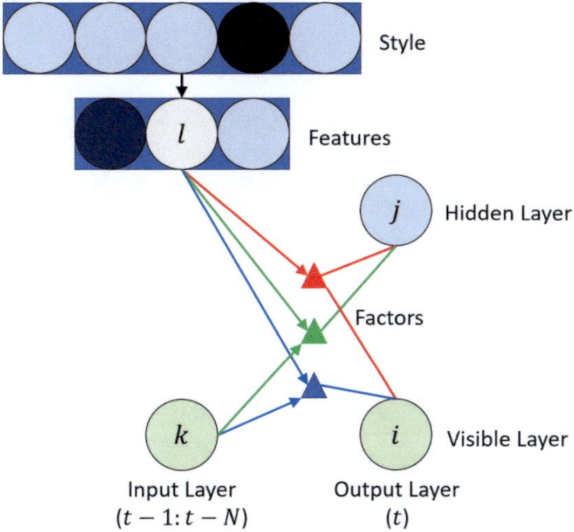

Fig. 13   Structure of an FCRBM

Figure 13 shows the structure of an FCRBM. Real style features are fed into the system. Those are connected to the visible and hidden entities via three factors. The factorized three-way interactions allow the style features to influence three different sets of pairwise interactions. The model defines a probability distribution over v_t and h_t, depending on the past N observations, the past visible layers $v_{<t}$, and the model parameters θ. The distribution depends on the style labels y_t. Similar to a CRBM, binary stochastic hidden units and real visible units with additive Gaussian noise are employed here as well. To simplify the notation, set $\sigma_i = 1$. The loss function is given by

$$E\left(v_t, h_t \mid v_{<t}, y_t, \theta\right) = \frac{1}{2} \sum_i \left(\hat{a}_{i,t} - v_{i,t}\right)^2 - \sum_f \sum_{ijl} W_{if}^v\, W_{jf}^h\, W_{lf}^z\, v_{i,t}\, h_{j,t}\, z_{l,t} - \sum_j \hat{b}_{j,t}\, h_{j,t} \quad (16)$$

The three terms in Eq. 16 correspond to the three submodels in Figure 13. For each submodel, the previous weight matrix is replaced by three sets of weights that connect units to the factors. Those three submodels can have different numbers of factors. These are indexed by f, m, and n. The dynamic biases are

$$\hat{a}_{i,t} = a_i + \sum_m A_{im}^v \sum_k A_{km}^{v<t}\, v_{k,<t} \sum_l A_{lm}^z\, z_{l,t} \quad (17)$$

$$\hat{b}_{j,t} = b_j + \sum_n B_{jn}^h \sum_k B_{kn}^{v<t}\, v_{k,<t} \sum_l B_{ln}^z\, z_{l,t} \quad (18)$$

The dynamic components of these equations represent the total input to the visible and hidden units via the factors. The total input is a three-way product of the input of the factors from the past and the style features as well as the weights of the factors of the visible and hidden units. The dynamic biases include static components, a and b. In order to calculate a good approximation of the gradients, the CD algorithm is used. The updates for all W, A and B parameters are built as follows:

$$\Delta X_{qr} \propto \sum_t \left(\langle \alpha_{q,t} \beta_{r,t} \gamma_{r,t} \rangle_0 - \langle \alpha_{q,t} \beta_{r,t} \gamma_{r,t} \rangle_K \right) \tag{19}$$

The units $\alpha_{q,t}(q \in i, j, k, l)$ are associated with the factor $r(r \in f, m, n)$ (related to the weight X_{qr}). The expectation related to the data distribution is denoted by $\langle \rangle_0$. In addition, $\langle \rangle_K$ is the expectation related to the joint distribution. The updates for the hidden and visible biases are the same as for the standard CRBM. The quality of the model can be evaluated using held-out frames. Accordingly, the root mean square error (RMSE) can be used as a metric. When modeling human motion, the FCRBM allows the style to change the effective weights of the network over discrete or real representations. Changing these style-based factors during generation can produce natural-looking transitions and enable interpolation and extrapolation of styles in the training data. Another advantage of FCRBM is that it is not dependent on the complete original data set. Only a few samples are needed for the initialization phase. Therefore, FCRBMs are less memory intensive. In addition, the training is linear with respect to the number of samples. As a consequence, FCRBMs can be scaled to larger data sets. By factorizing the three-way factors, the number of parameters can be reduced from $O\left(n^3\right)$ to $O\left(n^2\right)$. [8] [11] [12]

C. Recurrent Temporal Restricted Boltzmann Machines

The Recurrent Temporal Restricted Boltzmann Machine (RTRBM) is another type of RBM. It is an extension of the Temporal Restricted Boltzmann Machine (TRBM). In addition to its temporal property, RTRBMs contain a recurrent component. They are also used in the area of human motion sequence generation.

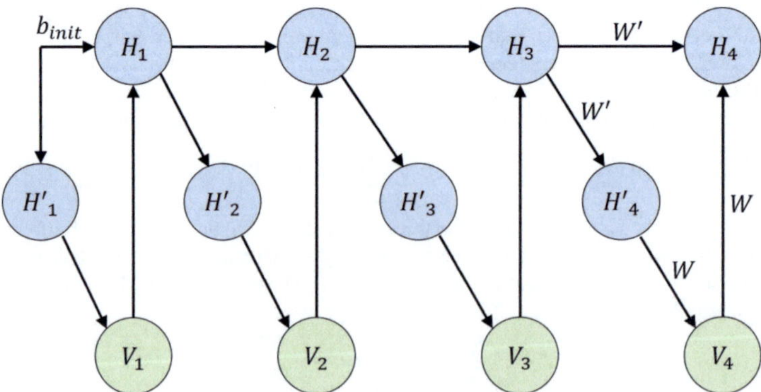

Fig. 14   Structure of an RTRBM

The structure of an RTRBM is simpler than that of a TRBM. More precisely, RTRBMs have no connections between those visible and hidden layers which are separated by more than one time interval. The structure of an RTRBM is illustrated in Figure 14. This means that the visible and hidden values at time t are conditionally independent of the visible values before time t and the hidden values before time $t - 1$, if the hidden values are given at time $t - 1$. The random variables H_t are real values, while the variables H_t' are binary values. The weight matrix W describes the influence between the visible and hidden units. The matrix W' weights the connections between the previous expected variables H_{t-1} and the variable H_t of the hidden units. RTRBMs use the expected variables for the hidden variables at time $t - 1$. However, the conditional distribution Q of the visible and hidden variables at time t is defined by their binary values H_t'. The conditional distribution $Q(V_t, H_t'|h_{t-1})$ is defined as follows:

$$Q\left(v_t, h_t' \mid h_{t-1}\right) = \frac{\exp\left(v_t^T W h_t' + v_t^T b_V + h_t'(b_H + W' h_{t-1})\right)}{Z(h_{t-1})} \tag{20}$$

Here, the variables b_V and b_H denote the biases of the visible and hidden units. The quantity Z denotes a normalization factor that ensures that Eq. 20 is a valid probability distribution. The RTRBM defines a probability distribution $Q\left(V_1^T, H_1^T\right)$ by the following equation:

$$Q\left(v_1^T, h_1^T\right) = \prod_{t=2}^{T} Q(v_t \mid h_{t-1}) Q(h_t \mid v_t, h_{t-1}) Q_0(v_1) Q_0(h_1 \mid v_1) \tag{21}$$

The parameters of an RTRBM can be trained over time by backpropagation, analogous to an RNN. In addition, the gradients from each time step are computed using the CD algorithm. The values to be expected of the hidden units are updated from r_{t-1} to r_t. These can be calculated by the following equation:

$$r_t = s\left(W v_t + b_H + W' r_{t-1}\right) \tag{22}$$

The RNN part has a pair of variables (v_t, r_t) $T_{t=1}$ at each time step, where v_t are the input variables and r_t are the hidden variables of the RNN. Here, s represents the logistic function. The evaluation metric is entirely qualitative, since computing the log-likelihood for a test set is not possible for both the TRBM and the RTRBM. An examination of the visible-to-hidden connection weights of the RTRBM reveals a number of hidden units that are not connected to visible units. These units have the most active hidden-to-hidden connections. Therefore, they must be used to transmit information over time. Overall, RTRBM achieves more natural results than TRBM. [8] [13]

D. Variational-Autoencoder Generative Adversarial Networks

The Variational Autoencoder Generative Adversarial Network (VAE-GAN) is a combination of two generative algorithms. It is composed of a VAE and a GAN.

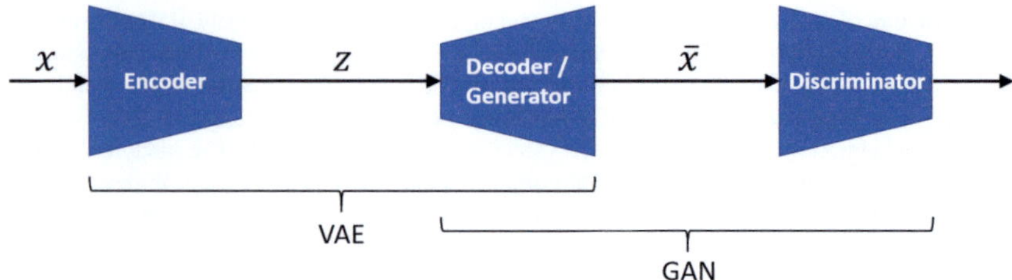

Fig. 15   Structure of a VAE-GAN

Figure 15 shows the connection of the VAE and GAN in series. The VAE contains an encoder and decoder. The encoder transforms the original data set (x) into a latent representation (z). The decoder transforms such latent representation into synthetic data ($\bar{x}$). The GAN completes the second half of the model with a generator and discriminator. Here, the generator is also the decoder of the VAE. Since the discriminator learns the main features of the input data, a more precise measure of reconstruction is recommended. More concretely, the distance between the original and generated data in the lth layer of the discriminator is used. By minimizing L_{Disl}, instead of element-wise reconstruction, and by additionally discriminating reconstructed data, VAE-GANs generate higher quality data than VAEs in general. VAE-GANs are trained by minimizing a triple criterion:

$$L = \beta L_{prior} + \gamma L_{Disl} + L_{GAN} \tag{23}$$

with

$$L_{prior} = -\mathbb{E}_{q(z|x)} \left[\log p(x|z) \right] \tag{24}$$

$$L_{Disl} = -\mathbb{E}_{q(z|x)} \left[\log p\left(Disc_l(x)|z \right) \right] \tag{25}$$

$$L_{GAN} = L^*_{GAN} + \log \left(1 - Disc(Dec(Enc(x))) \right) \tag{26}$$

Here, the regularization term in Eq. 24 promotes an encoding of the latent space. Eq. 25 provides a more accurate measure of the reconstructions in the first layer of the discriminator by the distance between the original and generated data. Eq. 26 provides additional discrimination of the reconstructed data, compared to the original data set. The encoder, decoder, generator, and discriminator are designed as a 4-layer 1D Convolutional Neural Network (CNN). Such VAE-GANs include 6 different hyperparameters in all. In more detail, these are given by the kernel size, mini-batch size, learning rate, momentum as well as the parameters β and γ. The kernel size is the size of the filter used by a CNN layer. The mini-batch size specifies the division of the entire training data set into smaller units. The factor β defines the independence of features in the latent space. The parameter γ defines the influence of the reconstructions with respect to the discriminator. The learning rate and the momentum are hyperparameters belonging to the Adams optimizer. The relu and sigmoid functions are used as activation functions. VAE-GANs can be validated explicitly. For example, the metrics Dynamic Time Warping (DTW) and the Structural Similarity Index (SSIM) can be used. [8] [14]

E. Recurrent-Conditional Generative Adversarial Networks

The Recurrent-Conditional Generative Adversarial Network (RCGAN) is a type of GAN consisting of recurrent and conditional parts. Typical RCGANs are made of a generator and a discriminator in the form of RNNs including LSTMs. The output is conditioned on an input vector y for both the generator and the discriminator. Thus, the conditional probability distribution $p(x|y)$ is learned. The corresponding minimax problem is defined by

$$\min_{G} \max_{D} \mathbb{E}_{x \sim p_{data}(x|y)} \left[\log D(x|y) \right] + \mathbb{E}_{z \sim p_z(z|y)} \left[\log(1 - D(G(z|y)|y)) \right] \tag{27}$$

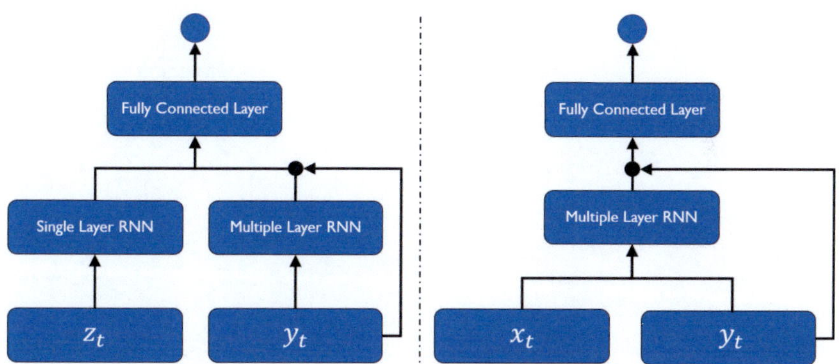

Fig. 16   Generator and Discriminator of an RCGAN

Figure 16 shows the structure of the network architectures of the generator and the discriminator. The generator consists of two RNN units. The first unit is assigned to the latent vector z_t and a conditional input is fed to the second unit. These two outputs are merged together with a bypass, starting from the conditional input y_t, and routed to a fully connected layer. The added bypass allows the generator to make predictions from both memory and current information. The entire output of the generator thereby forms a linear activation. By varying the network size and the size of z_t, a sensitive adjustment of the amount of noise applied to the output is possible. The discriminator, on the other hand, consists solely of an RNN-LSTM network. Two variables x_t and y_t are fed to them. The discriminator takes either a real or a synthetic time series as input (x_t) and provides as output at each time step a softmax probability that classifies whether the sample is real or not. The variable y_t describes the corresponding associated conditional input data. In this network, a bypass is applied again, starting from the variable y_t, to the fully-connected layer. These connections in both networks also result in a more stable and faster learning phase during training. According to the literature, two-layer RNNs are preferable in both the generator and discriminator. The Jensen–Shannon distance algorithm and root mean square error can be used to evaluate the time series generated. The RCGAN presented behaves relatively inaccurately at the beginning of the training phase. This is counteracted by longer training. In general, such an RCGAN constitutes a powerful model for the use case of safety-critixal driving data. RCGANs are able to handle time series of different lengths. The noise level can be tuned more precisely for the specific data distribution. Due to the memory property of the RNN-LSTM units used, RCGANs are able to generate numerically more stable time series and have the capability to learn the distribution of the original data set deeply. [8] [15] [16] [18]

F. Time-Series Generative Adversarial Networks

The Time-Series Generative Adversarial Network (TimeGAN) is a type of GAN specifically designed to generate time series of high quality. It is a combination of an embedding network and a generic network. Figure 17 shows the structure of the TimeGAN graphically.

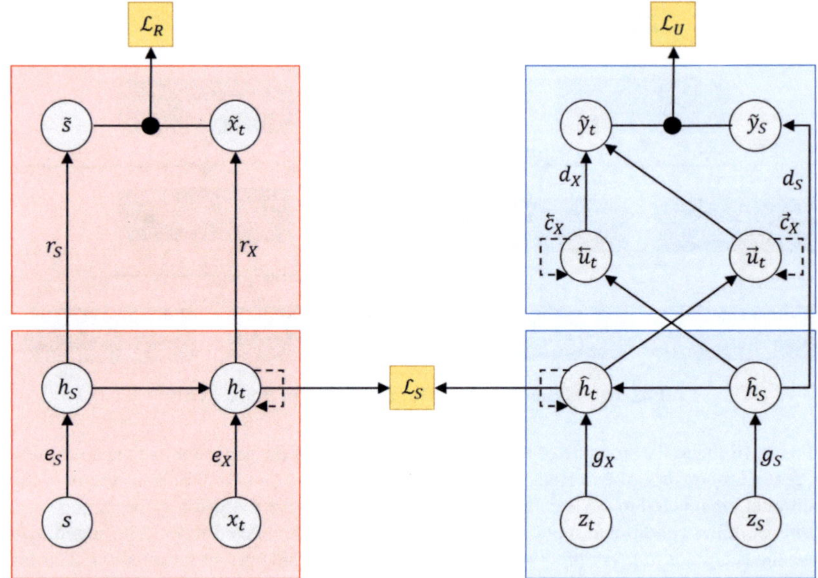

Fig. 17   Structure of a TimeGAN

It consists of four network components in all. Figure 17 shows an embedding and a recovery function on the left hand side. On the right hand side, a generator and discriminator are shown. The solid lines indicate the application of functions during the feed forward phase, the dashed lines indicate the recurrences, and the orange lines indicate the computation of loss functions applied. The auto-encoding components on the left hand side are trained together with the generic components on the right hand side. As a consequence, TimeGANs learn to encode features, generate representations, and iterate over time simultaneously. The latent space is provided by the embedding network. Therefore, the generic network can operate in the sub-space provided accordingly. The dynamic behaviour for both real and synthetic data are balanced by supervised loss. The embedding and recovery functions allow the generic network to learn the underlying temporal dynamics of the data by considering a low-dimensional representation between the features and the latent space. The latent vector spaces are denoted by H_S and H_X. The feature spaces are denoted by S and X. The embedding function e is implemented using a recurrent network. Here, e_S is an embedding network for static features and e_X for temporal features. The recovery function r reconstructs both static and temporal data based on the feature representations s and x_t. Here, r is implemented as a feed forward network, where r_S and r_X are so-called recovery networks for static and temporal embeddings.

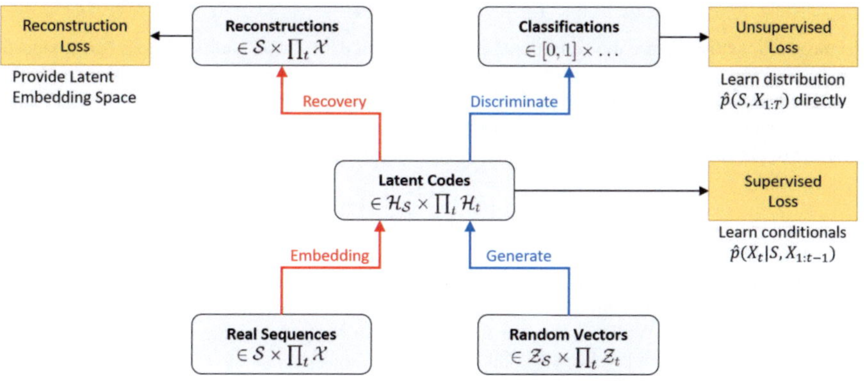

Fig. 18   Block diagram of a TimeGAN

The generator is directly connected to the embedding space (see Figure 18). Random vectors are fed to the latent space by the vector spaces Z_S and Z_X. The generating function g receives a tuple of static and temporal random vectors for mapping the latent space synthesized. The generator g is implemented as a recurrent network. Here, g_S represents a generator network for static features and g_X for temporal features. The random vector z_S can be sampled from a distribution function of choice, where z_t follows a stochastic process. The Gaussian distribution or Wiener process is used for this purpose. The discriminator is associated with the embedding space. The discriminator function d receives the static and temporal data and provides as an output classifications by $\tilde{y}_S$ and $\tilde{y}_t$. The discriminator d is implemented by a bidirectional recurrent network with a feed forward output layer. The notation $\tilde{h}_*$ indicates whether the embedded data are real (h_*) or synthetic ($\hat{h}_*$). Similarly, the notation $\tilde{y}_*$ denotes classifications of real (y_*) or synthetic ($\hat{y}_*$) data. The quantities $\overrightarrow{u}_t$ and $\overleftarrow{u}_t$ denote the sequences of hidden states during forward backward phase and $\overrightarrow{c}_X$ as well as $\overleftarrow{c}_X$ are recurrent functions. The functions d_S and d_X are classification functions of the output layer. The operation of the TimeGAN is described in the following in more detail. First, the embedding and reconstruction functions attempt to determine the most accurate reconstructions $\tilde{s}$ and $\tilde{x}_t$ from the original data s and x_t over their latent representations h_S and h_t. Therefore, likewise the first objective function of the reconstruction loss is given by:

$$\mathcal{L}_R = \mathbb{E}_{s,x1:T \sim p}\left[||s - \tilde{s}||_2 + \sum_t ||x_t - \tilde{x}_t||_2 \right] \tag{28}$$

The generator obtains, in an open-loop mode, synthetic embeddings $\hat{h}_S$ and $\hat{h}_{1:t-1}$. As a consequence, the next synthetic vector $\hat{h}_t$ can be calculated. Then, the gradients for the unsupervised loss are determined in order to maximize the likelihood for the discriminator and minimize it for the generator. This provides correct classifications for both the training data and the synthetic outputs of the generator. The unsupervised loss is described as follows:

$$\mathcal{L}_U = \mathbb{E}_{s,x1:T\sim p}\left[\log y_S + \sum_t \log y_t\right] + \mathbb{E}_{s,x1:T\sim \hat{p}}\left[\log(1 - \hat{y}_S) + \sum_t \log(1 - \hat{y}_t)\right] \quad (29)$$

To more efficiently capture the conditional distributions in the data, an additional loss is introduced for an additional learning. Here, the original data is used as supervised once in order to obtain further information from the training data. It is alternately trained in closed-loop mode, where the generator receives sequences of embeddings of the real data $h_{1:t-1}$ to generate the next latent vector. The use of the maximum-Likelihood approach yields the supervised loss in the following:

$$\mathcal{L}_S = \mathbb{E}_{s,x1:T\sim p}\left[\sum_t ||h_t - g_X(h_S, h_{t-1}, z_t)||_2\right] \quad (30)$$

In general, at each step of the training sequence, the difference between the actual latent vector of the next step from the embedding function and the synthetic latent vector of the next step from the generator is evaluated. While $\mathcal{L}_U$ pushes the generator to produce realistic sequences, $\mathcal{L}_S$ further ensures that the generator produces similar transitions.

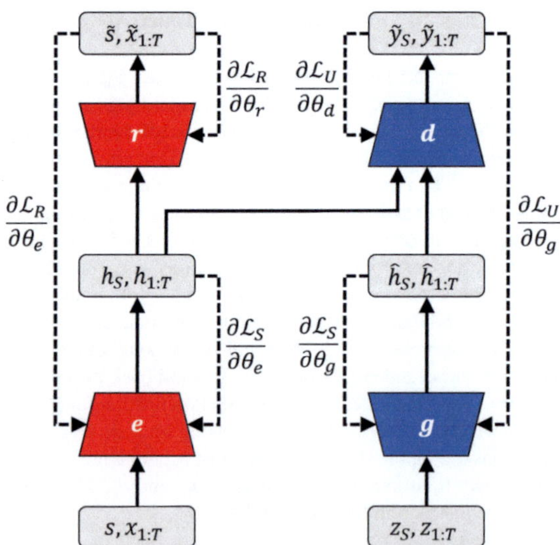

Fig. 19 Training scheme of a TimeGAN

Figure 19 shows the detailed procedure of the training approach. The parameters θ_e, θ_r, θ_g, and θ_d therein denote, respectively, the embedding, reconstruction, generator, and discriminator networks. The reconstruction loss and the supervised loss are trained as follows:

$$\min_{\theta_e,\theta_r}(\lambda\mathcal{L}_S + \mathcal{L}_R) \tag{31}$$

Here, λ is a hyperparameter. It was introduced to balance both losses $\mathcal{L}_S$ and $\mathcal{L}_R$. In order to support the generator's learning temporal relationships from the data, the embedding process is actively conditioned. Then, the generator and discriminator networks are trained:

$$\min_{\theta_g}(\eta\mathcal{L}_S + \max_{\theta_d}\mathcal{L}_U) \tag{32}$$

The size η is another hyperparameter. It was introduced to balance both losses $\mathcal{L}_S$ and $\mathcal{L}_U$. As a consequence, the generator minimizes the supervised loss also. By combining the embedding network with the generic network, TimeGANs are simultaneously trained to encode feature vectors, generate latent representations, and iterate over time. Finally, the entire network is generalized, where both static and time series can be generated simultaneously. For a qualitative evaluation of the data, both the t-SNE and PCA approaches can be applied in order to visualize how well the generated distributions resemble the original distributions. A post hoc classifier can be used in order to distinguish between real and generated sequences. In addition, by applying the Train on Synthetic, Test on Real (TSTR) framework to the prediction task of sequences, it is possible to evaluate how well the generated data inherits the predictive properties of the original data. TimeGANs represent a novel framework for time series generation. It combines the versatility of the unsupervised GAN approach with the control of conditional temporal dynamics provided by supervised autoregressive models. Further, the joint training of the embedding network with the generic networks continually increases the generative goodness. [8] [17]

VI. Recommendation

Various generative algorithms can be used to generate safety-critical driving data. With respect to time series-based data, the aforementioned generative algorithms can be used for this purpose. TimeGANs generate synthetic data of higher quality compared to other generative algorithms in terms both discriminative (post hoc classification error) and predictive (mean absolute error) senses. Similarly, the synthetic data evaluated by t-SNE shows a significantly more accurate match compared to the original data with respect to the algorithms of the aforementioned benchmark. [8] [17]

In the following, the quality of the data generation of a TimeGAN is shown for the use case of safety-critical driving data. In this context, an emergency braking serves as the safety-critical driving scenario. Figure 20 shows the distance traveled in the longitudinal direction over time during the braking process. The original data set is in blue and the generated data set is in red. The blue lines are created based on considering the kinematic equations described in [19]. The red lines correspond to the data generated by the TimeGAN. Overall, there is a strong correspondence between the original and generated data sets. In addition, the generated data set provides an appropriate variance. So, besides the original data set, further time series could be created which also make up an emergency braking scenario in general. As a consequence, the overall size of the data set of an underlying safety-critical driving scenario can be increased in such a manner.

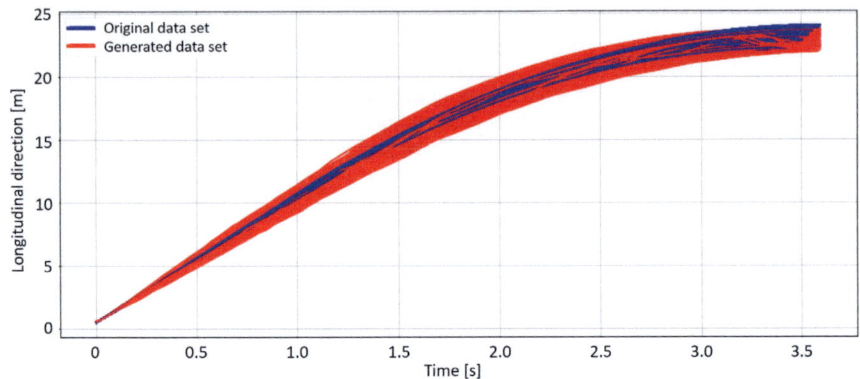

Fig. 20   TimeGAN generated data of an emergency braking movement

VII. Conclusion

Various generative algorithms can be used to generate safety-critical driving data in the field of autonomous driving. In this context, a novel taxonomy for the generation of time series was presented and the corresponding generative algorithms were described in more detail. In particular, the TimeGAN variant is recommended due to its accuracy compared to generative algorithms on the same benchmark. As a consequence, TimeGANs can be used in order to increase the amount of time series corresponding to safety-critical driving scenarios.

References

[1] ASSOCIATION FOR SAFE INTERNATIONAL ROAD TRAVEL (ASIRT), 2021. ROAD SAFETY FACTS [online]. Maryland: ASIRT, 2021 [Accessed on: 02.06.2021]. Available at: `https://www.asirt.org/safe-travel/road-safety-facts`

[2] POLICYADVICE, 2021. How Many People Die in Car Accidents? [online]. Kopestinsky, A., 27.02.2021 [Accessed on: 02.06.2021]. Available at: `https://policyadvice.net/insurance/insights/car-accidents`

[3] UNITED NATIONS, 2020. At Stockholm road safety summit, UN officials join global call to end 'scourge' of preventable deaths [online]. UN News, 19.02.2020 [Accessed on: 02.06.2021]. Available at: `https://news.un.org/en/story/2020/02/1057721`

[4] WORLD HEALTH ORGANIZATION, 2020. Road traffic injuries [online]. Ort: World Health Organization, 07.02.2020 [Accessed on: 02.06.2021]. Available at: `https://www.who.int/news-room/fact-sheets/detail/road-traffic-injuries`

[5] U.S. DEPARTMENT OF HEALTH HUMAN SERVICES, 2020. Road Traffic Injuries and Deaths - A Global Problem [online]. Centers for Disease Control and Prevention, National Center for Injury Prevention and Control, 14.12.2020 [Accessed on: 02.06.2021]. Available at: `https://www.cdc.gov/injury/features/global-road-safety/index.html`

[6] CORLITO, Roberto, 2020. Analyse und Gegenüberstellung von geeigneten Evaluierungstechniken zur Validierung von generativen Algorithmen im Kontext der Bereitstellung von zeitreihen-bezogenen Daten [Bachelorarbeit]. Esslingen: Hochschule Esslingen

[7] KREISS, Jens-Peter und Georg NEUHAUS, 2006. Einführung in die Zeitreihenanalyse. 1. Auflage. Berlin Heidelberg: Springer-Verlag. ISBN 978-3-540-33571-9

[8] ÜN, Eugen, 2020. Analyse von geeigneten generativen Algorithmen zur Generierung von sicherheitskritischen Fahrszenarien im Bereich des autonomen Fahrens [Bachelorarbeit]. Esslingen: Hochschule Esslingen

[9] RASCHKA, Sebastian und Vahid Mirjalili, 2019. Python Machine Learning: Machine Learning and Deep Learning with Python, scikit-learn, and TensorFlow 2. 3. Auflage. Birmingham: Packt Publishing. ISBN 9781789955750

[10] HINDUPUR, Avinash, 2018. The GAN Zoo [online]. GitHub, 30.09.2018 [Accessed on: 02.06.2021]. Available at: `https://github.com/hindupuravinash/the-gan-zoo`

[11] Taylor, G. W., Hinton, G. E., Roweis, S. (2007). Modeling Human Motion Using Binary Latent Variables. In B. Schölkopf, J. Platt, T. Hoffman (Eds.), Advances in Neural Information Processing Systems (Vol. 19). MIT Press. `https://proceedings.neurips.cc/paper/2006/file/1091660f3dff84fd648efe31391c5524-Paper.pdf`

[12] Taylor, G. W., Hinton, G. E. (2009). Factored conditional restricted Boltzmann Machines for modeling motion style. ICML, 1025–1032. `https://doi.org/10.1145/1553374.1553505`

[13] Sutskever, I., Hinton, G. E., Taylor, G. W. (2009). The Recurrent Temporal Restricted Boltzmann Machine. In D. Koller, D. Schuurmans, Y. Bengio, L. Bottou (Eds.), Advances in Neural Information Processing Systems (Vol. 21). Curran Associates, Inc. `https://proceedings.neurips.cc/paper/2008/file/9ad6aaed513b73148b7d49f70afcfb32-Paper.pdf`

[14] Parthasarathy, D., Bäckström, K., Henriksson, J., Einarsdóttir, S. (2020). Controlled time series generation for automotive software-in-the-loop testing using GANs. 2020 IEEE International Conference On Artificial Intelligence Testing (AITest), 39–46. doi: 10.1109/AITEST49225

[15] H. Arnelid, E. L. Zec and N. Mohammadiha, "Recurrent Conditional Generative Adversarial Networks for Autonomous Driving Sensor Modelling," 2019 IEEE Intelligent Transportation Systems Conference (ITSC), 2019, pp. 1613-1618, doi: 10.1109/ITSC.2019.8916999

[16] Esteban, C., Hyland, S. L., Rätsch, G. (2017). Real-valued (Medical) Time Series Generation with Recurrent Conditional GANs. ArXiv, abs/1706.02633

[17] Yoon, J., Jarrett, D., van der Schaar, M. (2019). Time-series Generative Adversarial Networks. In H. Wallach, H. Larochelle, A. Beygelzimer, F. d'Alché Buc, E. Fox, R. Garnett (Eds.), Advances in Neural Information Processing Systems (Vol. 32). Curran Associates, Inc. `https://proceedings.neurips.cc/paper/2019/file/c9efe5f26cd17ba6216bbe2a7d26d490-Paper.pdf`

[18] Goodfellow, I., Pouget-Abadie, J., Mirza, M., Xu, B., Warde-Farley, D., Ozair, S., Courville, A., Bengio, Y. (2014). Generative Adversarial Nets. In Z. Ghahramani, M. Welling, C. Cortes, N. Lawrence, K. Q. Weinberger (Eds.), Advances in Neural Information Processing Systems (Vol. 27). Curran Associates, Inc. https://proceedings.neurips.cc/paper/2014/file/5ca3e9b122f61f8f06494c97b1afccf3-Paper.pdf

[19] SCHICK, Nico, 2020. Modeling of specific safety-critical driving scenarios for data synthesis in the context of autonomous driving software. In: Cuvillier Verlag [online]. 06.08.2020 [Accessed on: 02.06.2021]. Available at: https://cuvillier.de/de/shop/publications/8271-modeling-of-specific-safety-critical-driving-scenarios-for-data-synthesis-in-the-context-of-autonomous-driving-software